DISCLAIMER

Copyright © 2019 by Kids Learning Essentials
All rights reserved.

Cover and interior images copyright
Authoritative Content, LLC.

No part of this publication may be reproduced, stored in a retrieval system, or transmitted in any form by any means, electronic, mechanical photocopying, recording or otherwise, without the prior written permission of the publisher.

THIS BOOK BELONGS TO:
_____

_____

_____

B

B B B B B B

B B B B B B

B B B B B B

B B B B B B

B B B B B B

B B B B B B

B B B B B B

B B B B B B

B B B B B B
B B B B B B
B B B B B B
B B B B B B
B B B B B B
B B B B B B
B B B B B B
B B B B B B

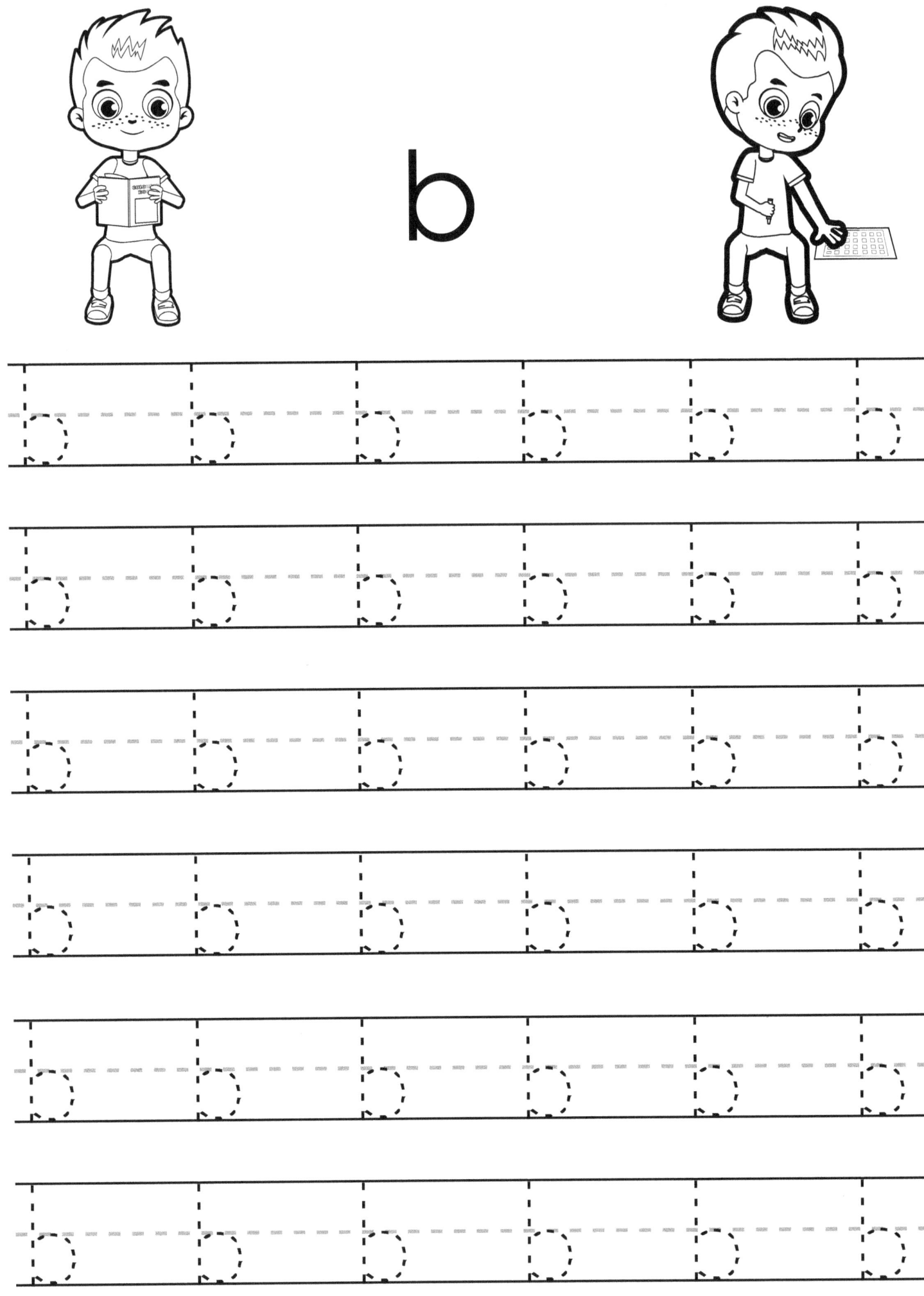

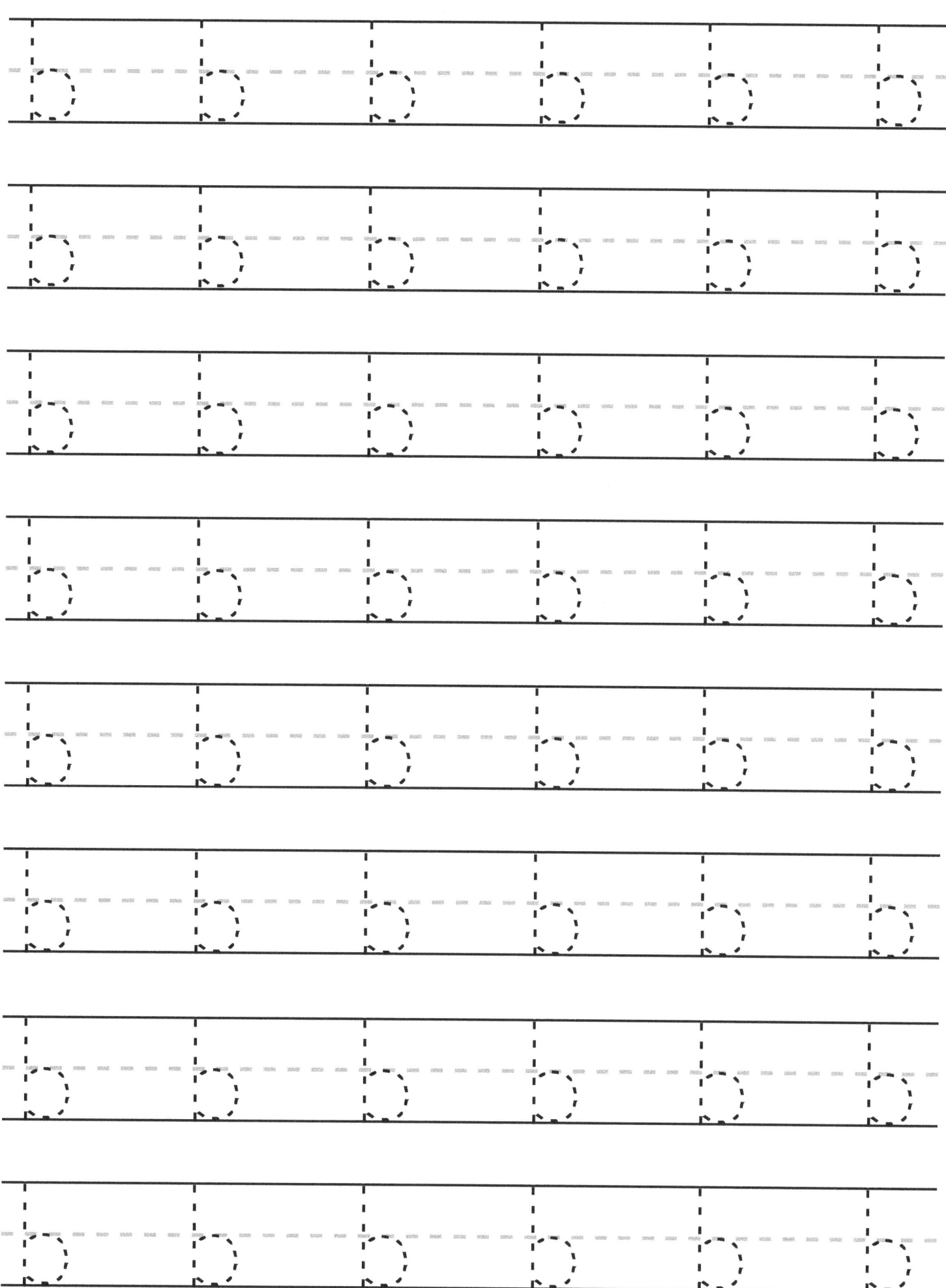

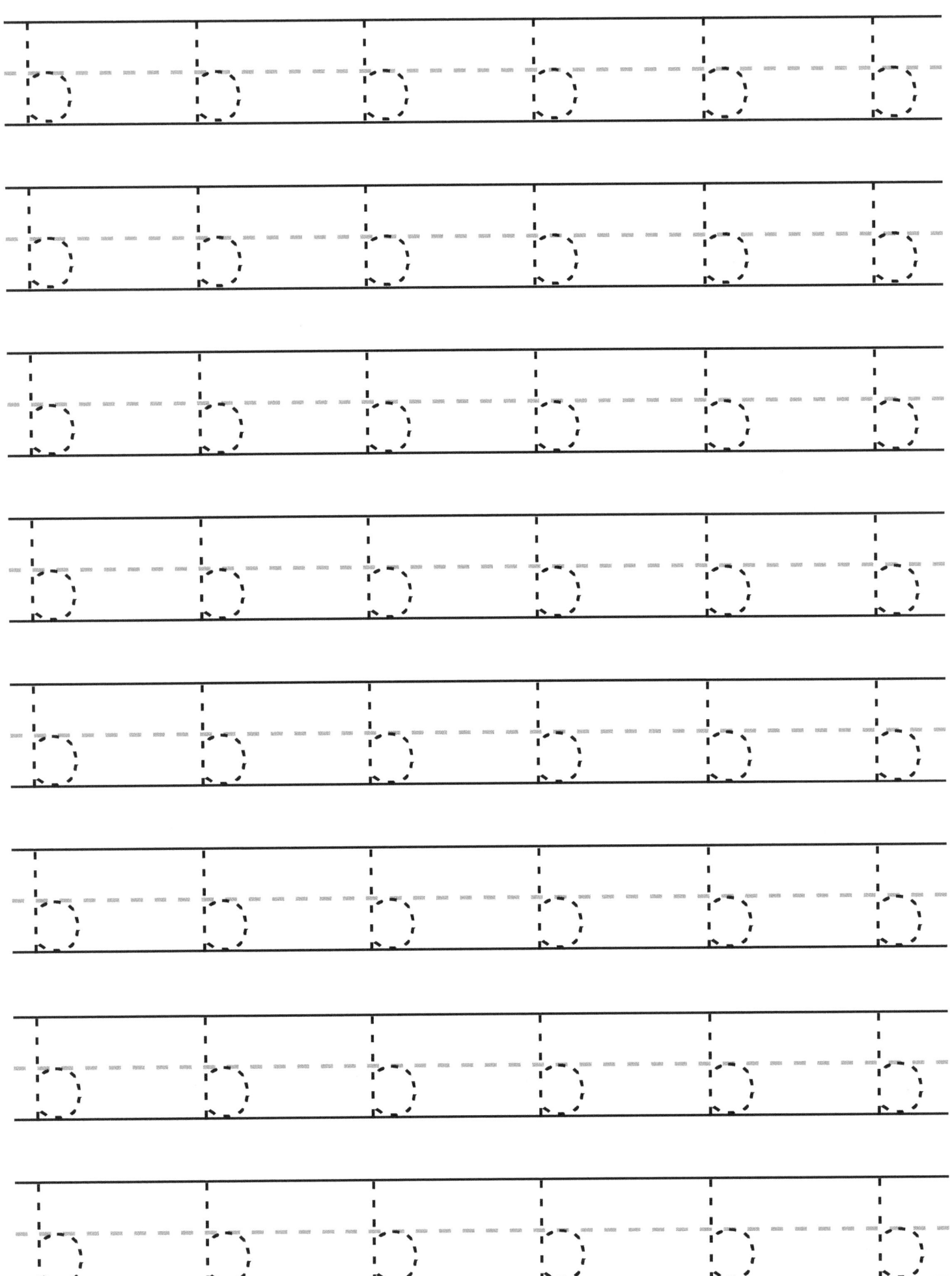

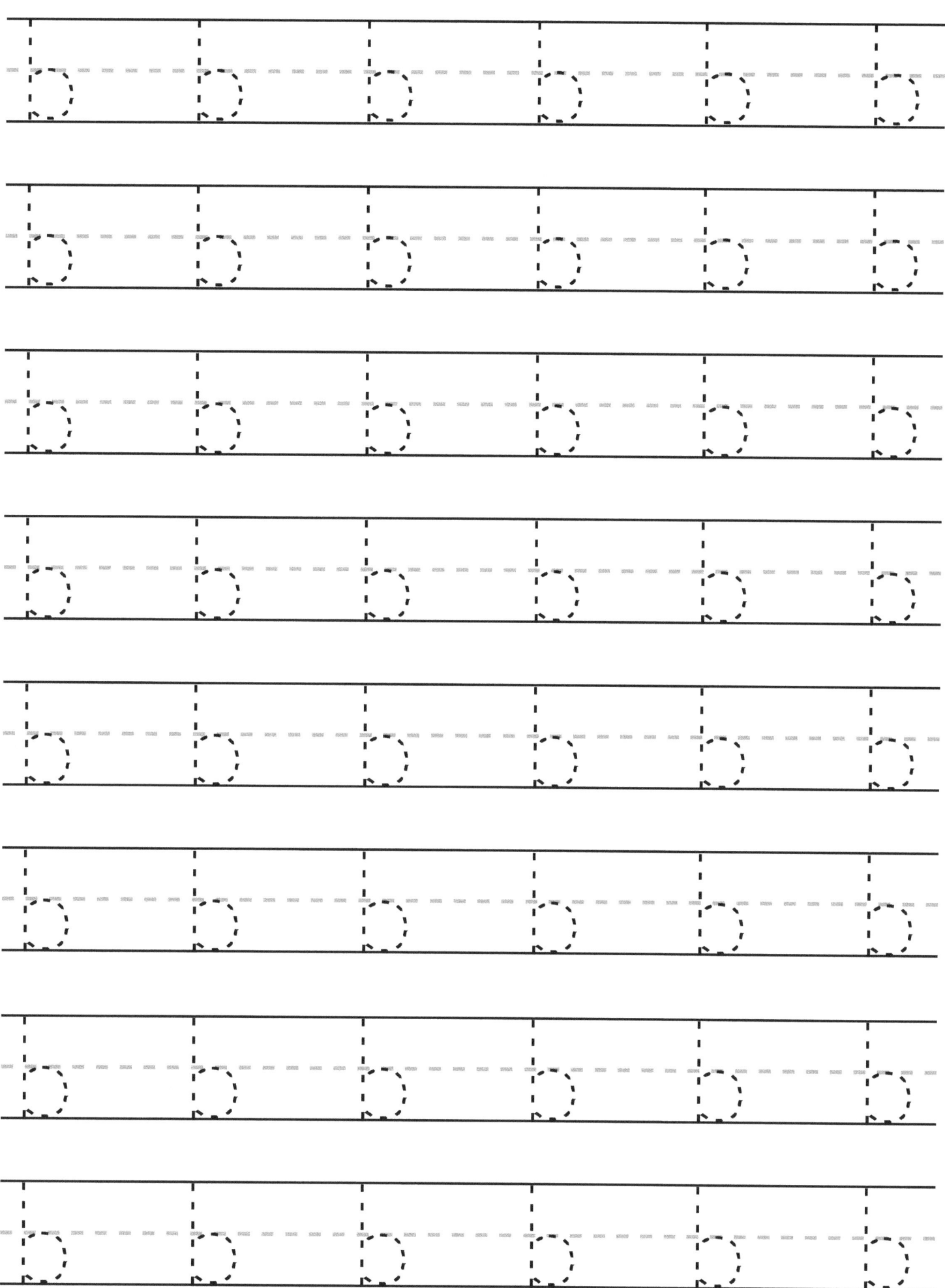

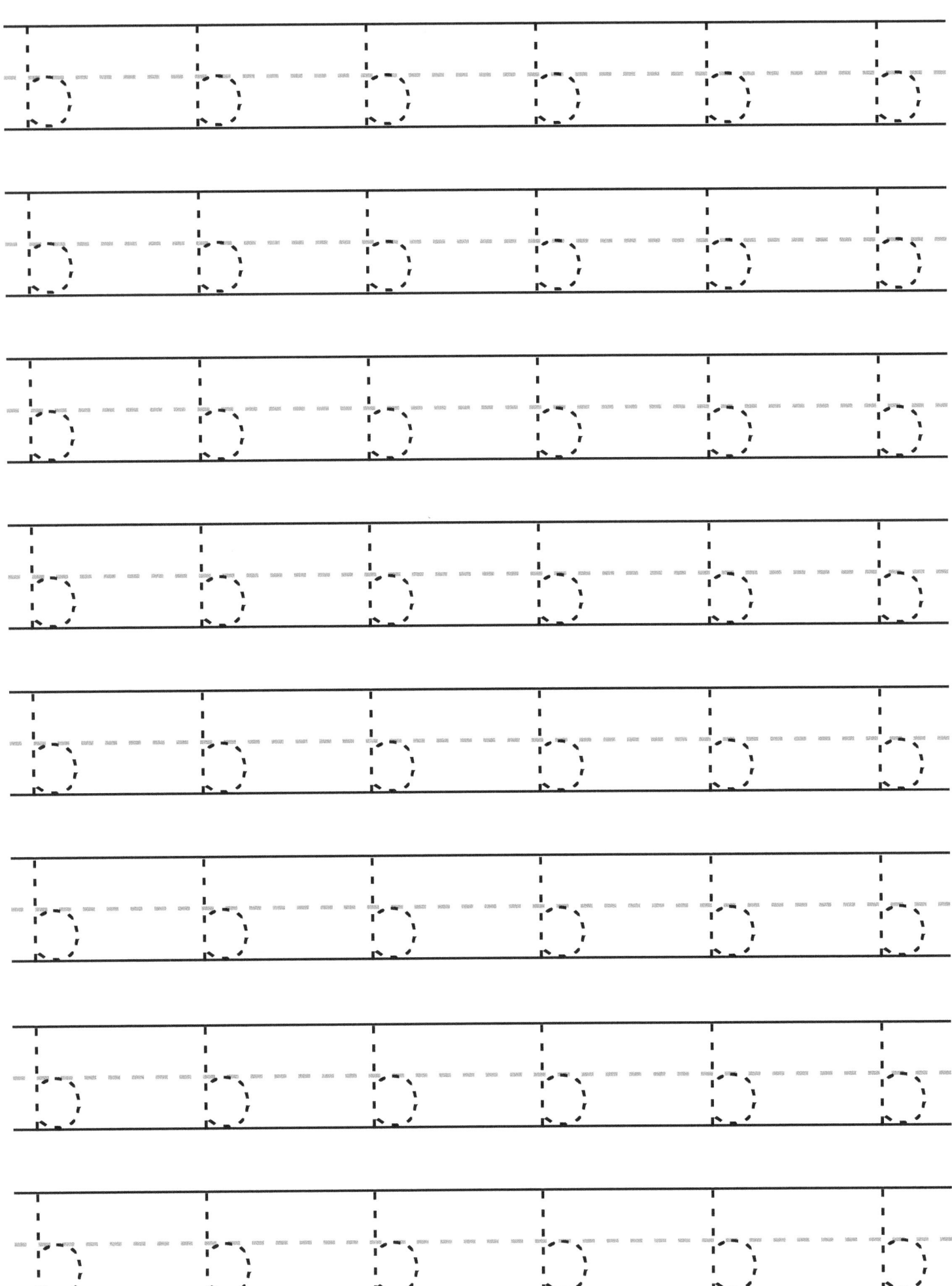

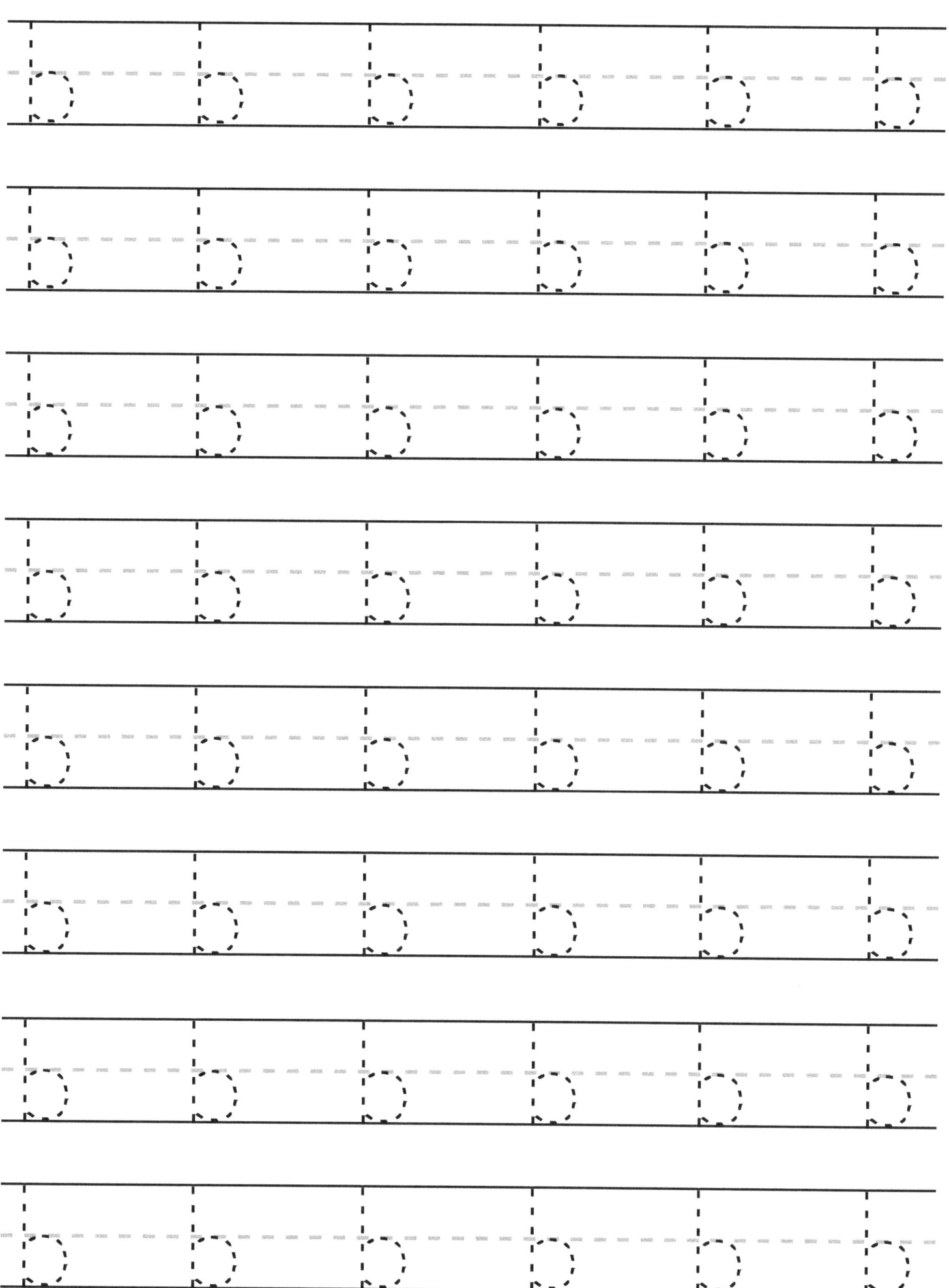

bird

bird bird bird

bird bird bird

bird bird bird

bird bird bird

bird bird bird

bird bird bird

bird bird bird

bird bird bird

bird bird bird

bird bird bird

bird bird bird

bird bird bird

bird bird bird

bird bird bird

bee

bee bee bee

bee bee bee

bee bee bee

bee bee bee

bee bee bee

bee bee bee

bee bee bee

bee bee bee

bee bee bee

bee bee bee

bee bee bee

bee bee bee

bee bee bee

bee bee bee

butterfly

butterfly butterfly

butterfly butterfly

butterfly butterfly

butterfly butterfly

butterfly butterfly

butterfly butterfly

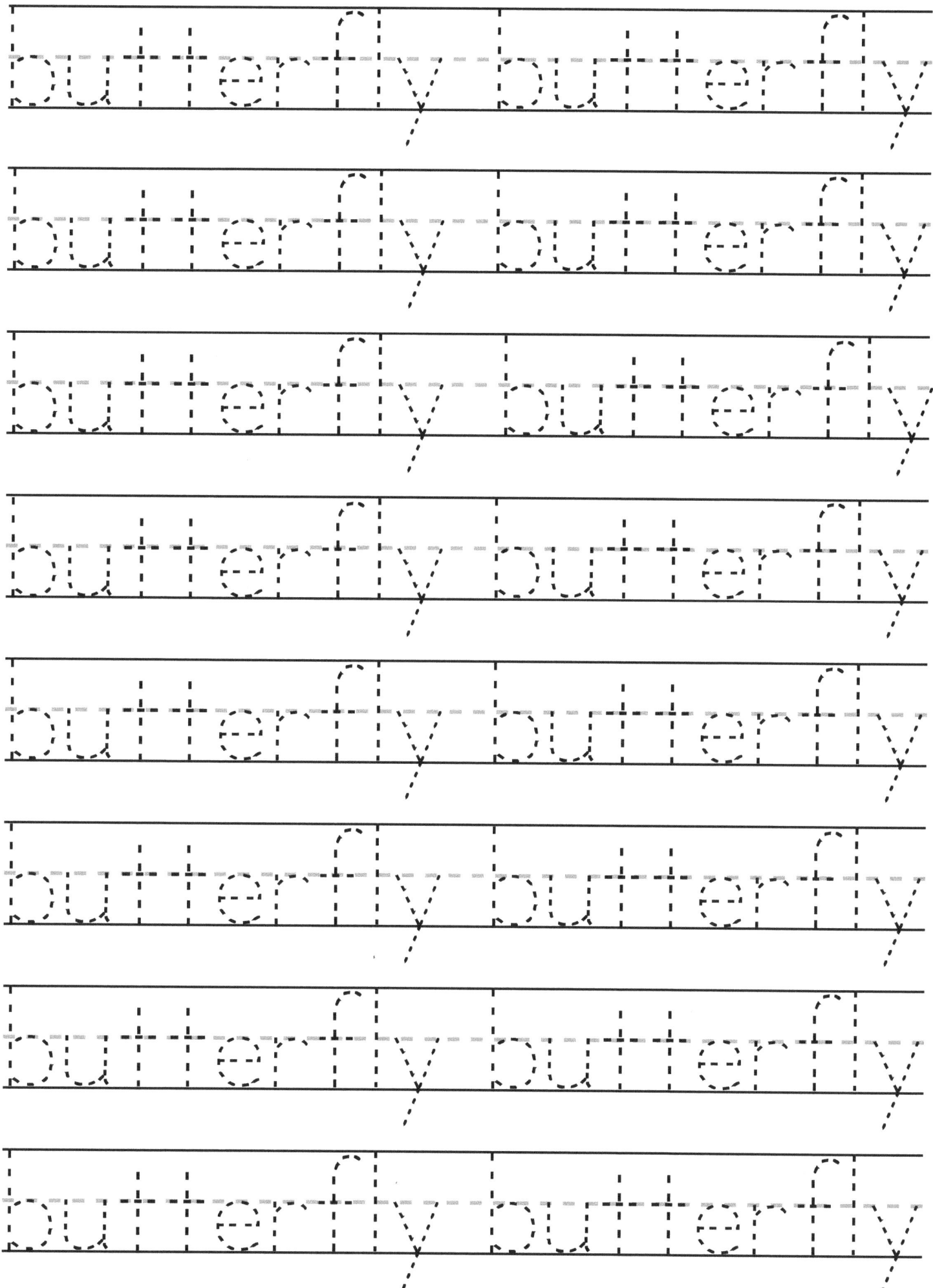

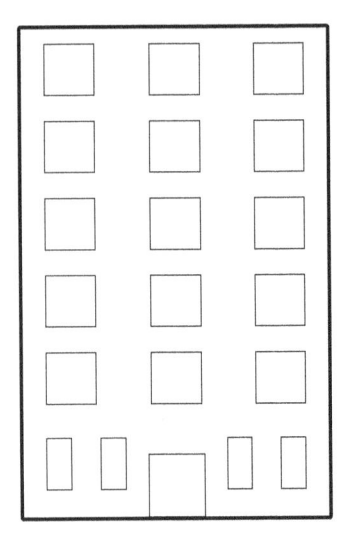

building

building　building

building　building

building　building

building　building

building　building

building　building

building building

building building

building building

building building

building building

building building

building building

building building

beach ball

beach ball

beach ball

beach ball

beach ball

beach ball

beach ball

beach ball

beach ball

beach ball

beach ball

beach ball

beach ball

beach ball

beach ball

book

book	book	book
book	book	book
book	book	book
book	book	book
book	book	book
book	book	book

book book book

book book book

book book book

book book book

book book book

book book book

book book book

book book book

balloons

balloons balloons

balloons balloons

balloons balloons

balloons balloons

balloons balloons

balloons balloons

balloons balloons

balloons balloons

balloons balloons

balloons balloons

balloons balloons

balloons balloons

balloons balloons

balloons balloons

Color the pictures that start with "b".

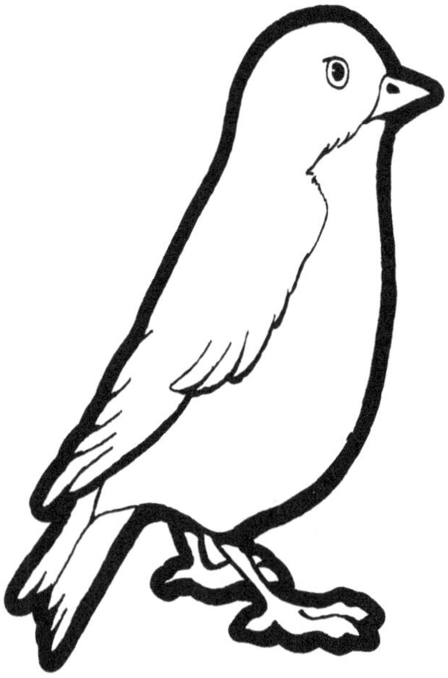

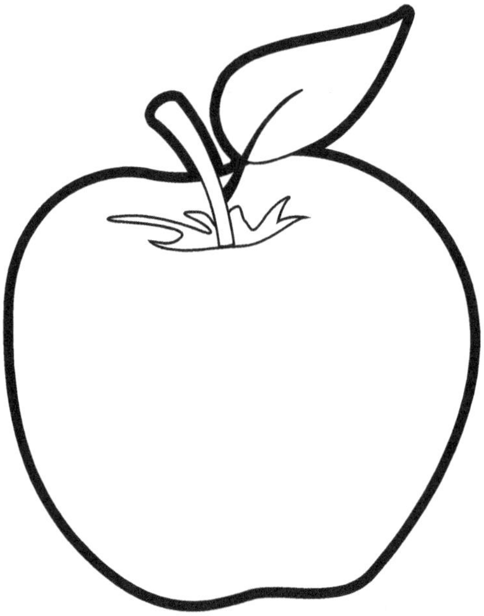

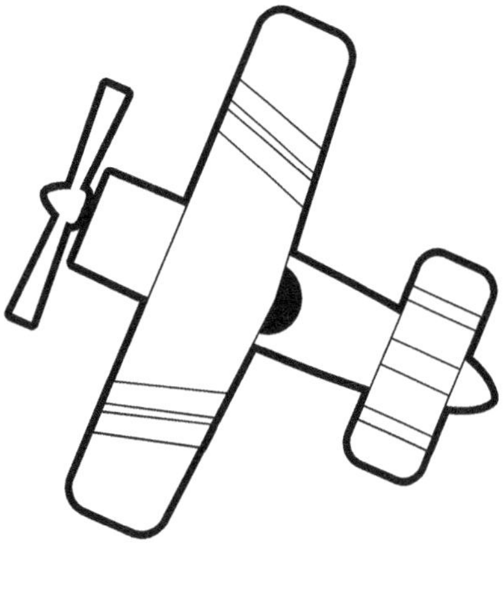

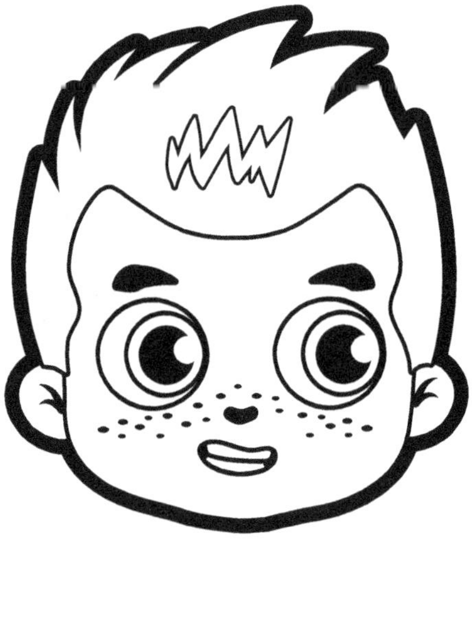

Color the pictures that start with "b".

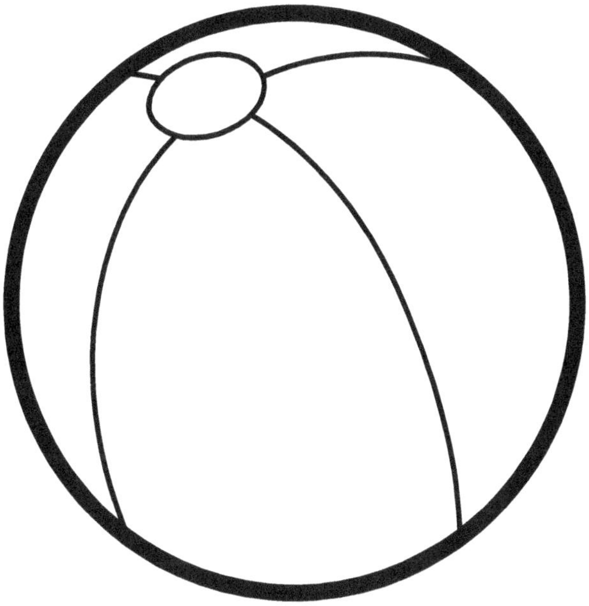

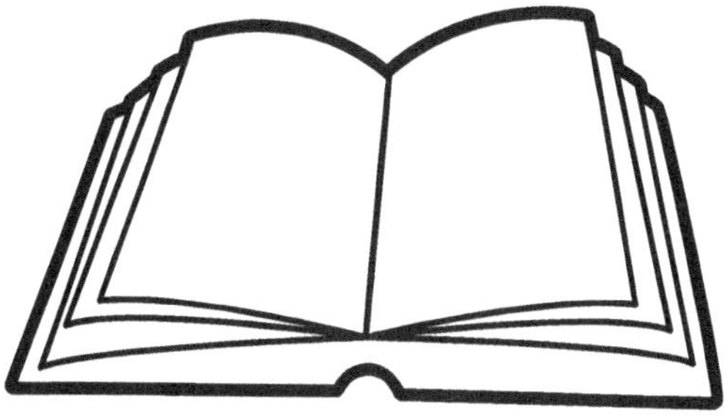

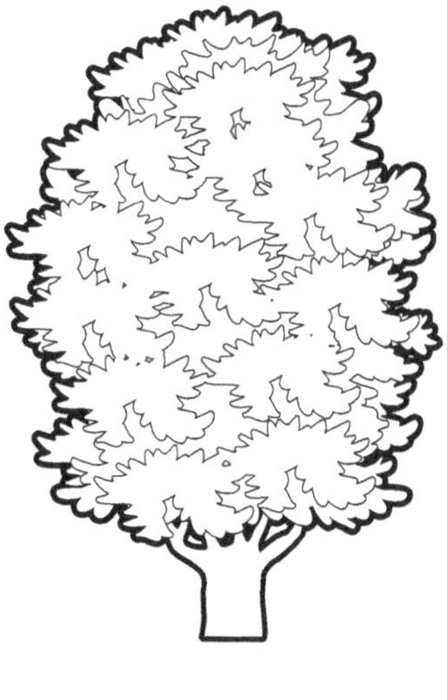

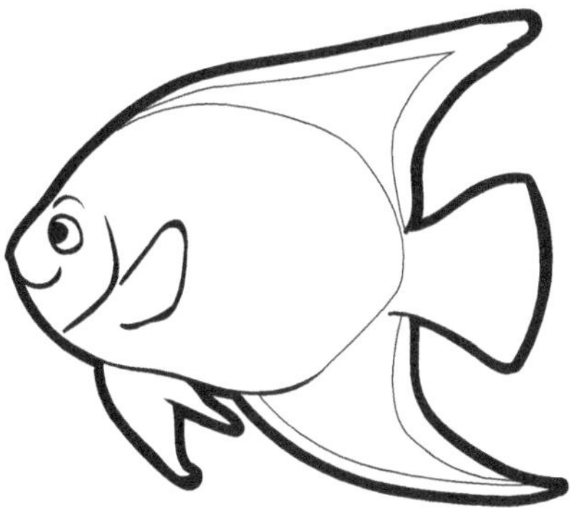

B Dot the B's.

P	G	B	B	A
Z	B	M	B	A
N	D	B	O	W

b Dot the b's.

b	p	l	j	n
g	b	r	b	b
p	x	g	b	b

Help Brandon Find The Words That Start With

Bb

Find the words that start with Bb
Color or Dot each word.

horse	but	color	an	how	big
here	and	book	soon	all	house
bird	and	plant	bird	says	want
house	bee	want	horse	color	each
bear	apple	how	but	bird	how

book	all	here	bear	here	an
each	here	up	want	want	how
want	all	want	how	bird	be
want	want	big	how	color	each
all	want	big	bunny	but	want
an	bird	bear	up	house	here
all	horse	hay	bunny	bee	horse
all	here	big	be	want	be
and	bunny	apple	book	plant	bird
plant	plant	color	how	color	all

Draw a line from each picture to the matching word.

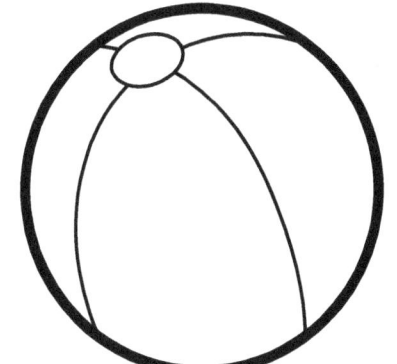

bird

butterfly

bee

beach ball

Draw a line from each picture to the matching word.

balloons

building

book

Brandon

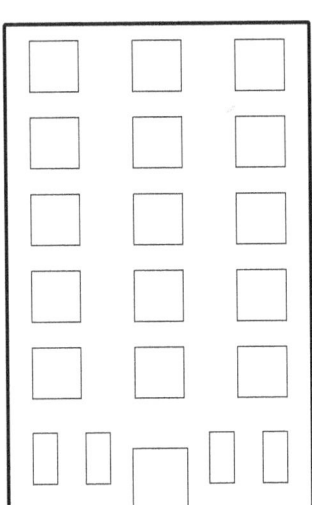

Circle the images that start with "B"

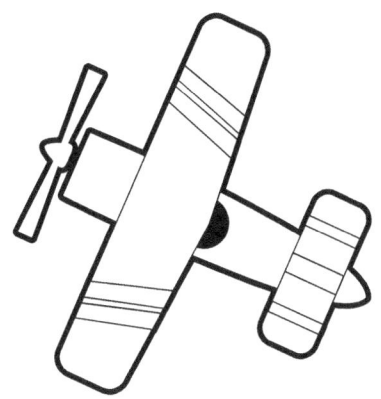

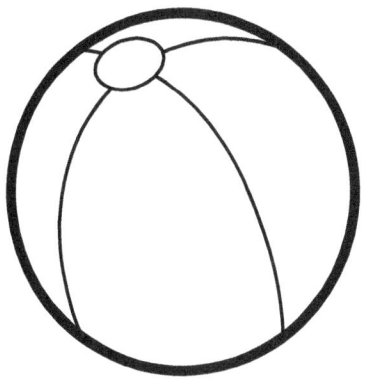

Circle the images that start with "B"

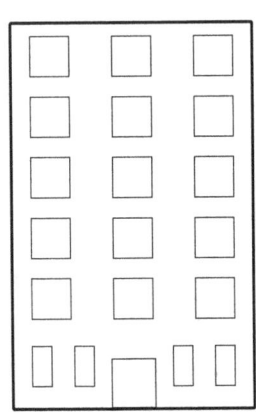

Fill in the missing letter for each word.

 _ird

 _utterfly

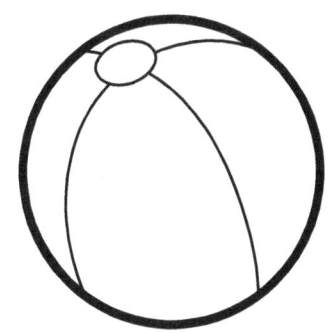 _each ball

 _ee

Fill in the missing letter for each word.

 _alloons

 _ook

 _ear

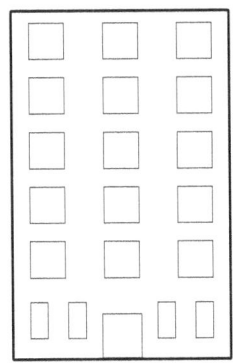 _uilding

Uppercase Letter Maze 'Bb'

Help Brandon find Benny by following the letter B through the maze.

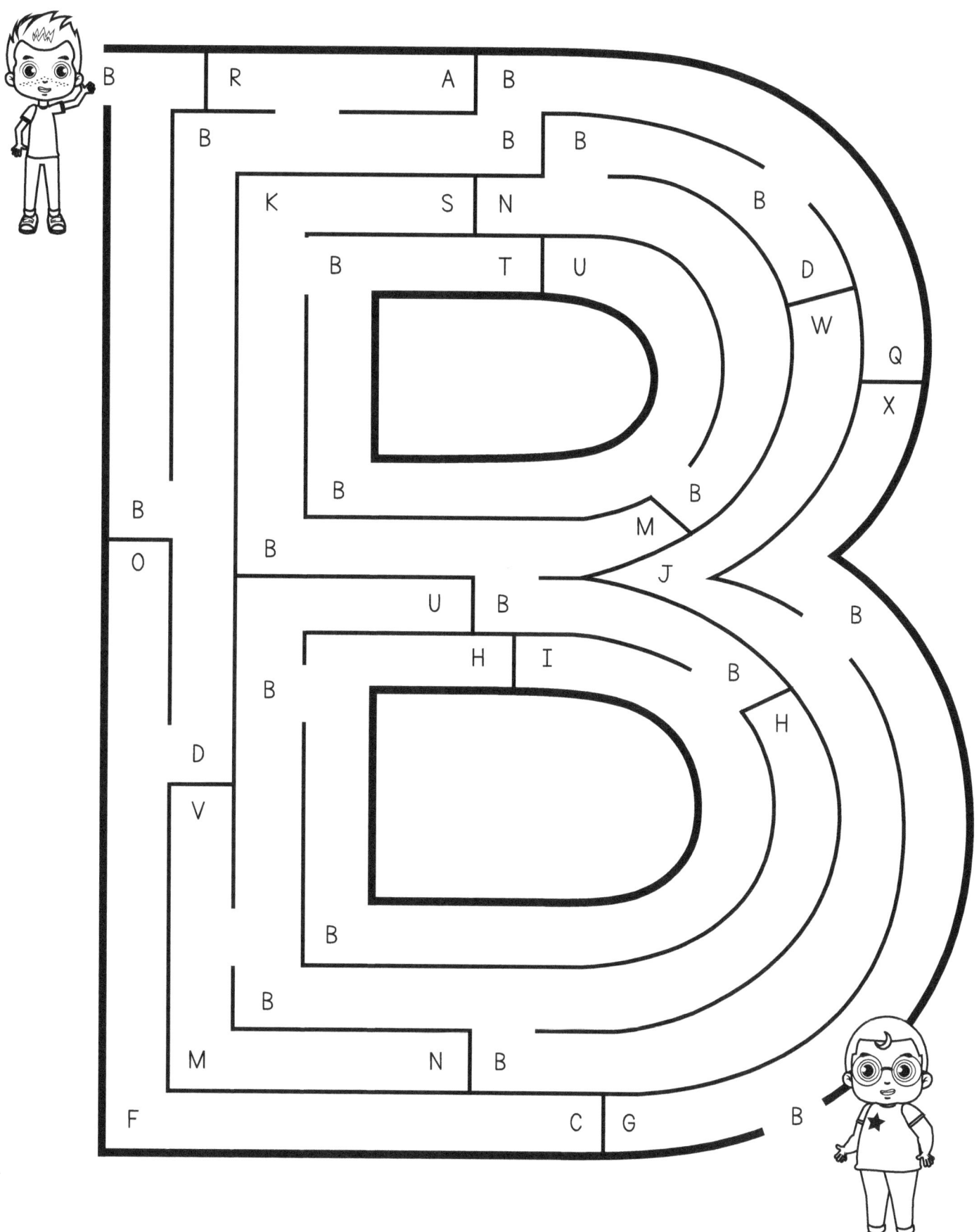

JOIN OUR VIP CLUB

Get **Free** Printables

Come and be a part of our learning family!

When you join the VIP Learning Essentials club, you'll get access to the following additional benefits:

- Unique printable pages based on our stories
- Early access to new book releases
- Discounts on new story and workbook releases
- Access to VIP only sales

With more writing book releases just around the corner, you won't want to miss out!

Entry to the club is simple: all you have to do is go to https://kidslearningessentials.com/join-our-vip-club and click the button that says "Click here to subscribe" and then fill out the form that pops up. You will immediately receive a confirmation email followed by your first set of VIP pages!

LEARN MORE AT
KIDSLEARNINGESSENTIALS.COM

GIVE US YOUR REVIEW!

Your thoughts and feedback on our alphabet books are not only important to us, but they are also essential in helping us to improve the quality of our products and grow our brand. So please feel free to let us, and other learners as well, know what you think!

To leave us a review, go to:

https://store.kidslearningessentials.com/

and click "Write a review" in the Customer Reviews section, which is just beneath every product description. From there you will be able to enter your name, email, rating and your review.

We appreciate your honest feedback.

VISIT US AT
KIDSLEARNINGESSENTIALS.COM